Contents

Counting to 20

Match the numbers to the insects.

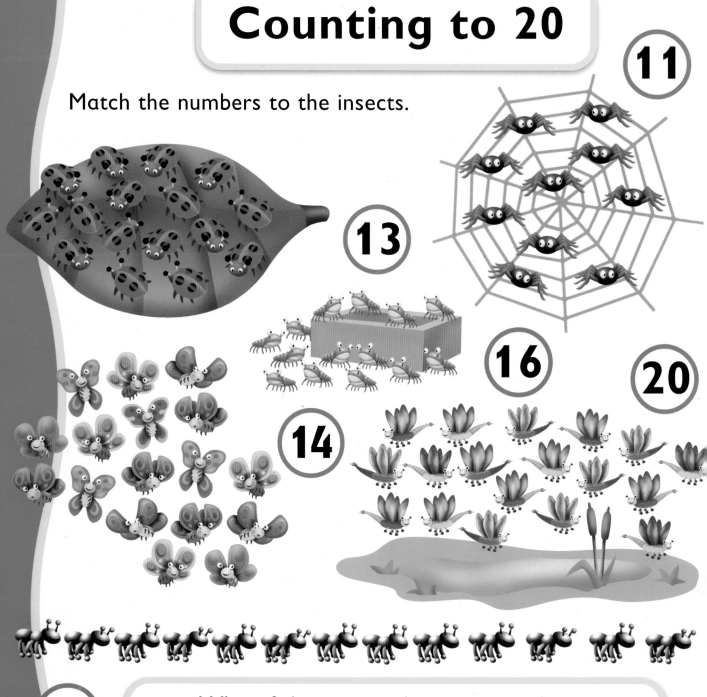

11

13

16

20

14

19

What if there were 1 more in each set.
How many would there be then? How many
would there be if there were 1 fewer in each set?

4

Maths Club
MAKING PROGRESS

Using Numbers

Ann Montague-Smith

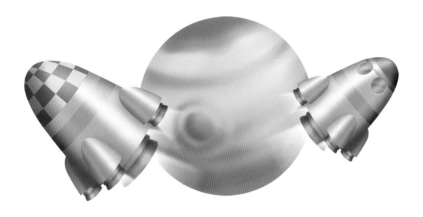

QED Publishing

First published in the UK in 2005 by
QED Publishing
A Quarto Group company
226-236 City Road
London EC1V 2TT

www.qed-publishing.co.uk

A Catalogue record for this book is available from the British Library.

ISBN 1 84538 427 X

Written by Ann Montague-Smith
Designed and edited by The Complete Works
Illustrated by Peter Lawson
Photography by Steve Lumb

Publisher Steve Evans
Creative Director Louise Morley
Editorial Manager Jean Coppendale

Printed and bound in China

With thanks to:

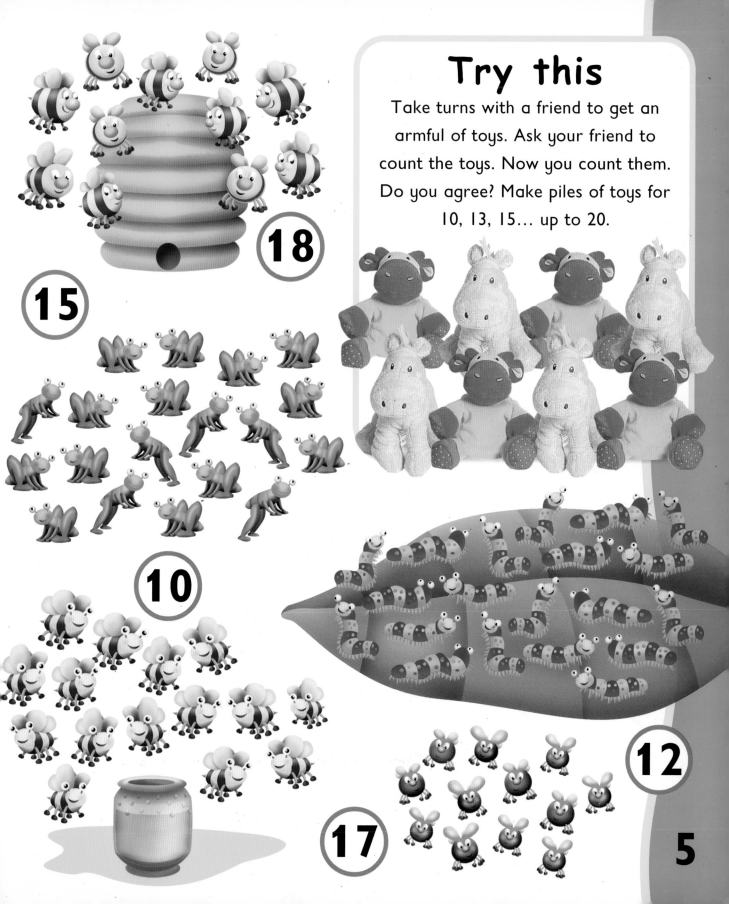

Try this

Take turns with a friend to get an armful of toys. Ask your friend to count the toys. Now you count them. Do you agree? Make piles of toys for 10, 13, 15... up to 20.

18

15

10

12

17

5

You will need a pile of 30 counters. Take a big handful of counters from the pile and put them onto the carpet below. Guess how many there are. Now count them to check.

6

Do this 5 more times.

Now try this

Use handfuls of straws instead of counters. Estimate and count to check. Do this 5 more times.

7

Numbers to 30

Play this game with a friend. You will need a 1-6 dice and a counter each. Take turns to roll the dice. Move your counter that number of spaces. Say the number where your counter lands. The winner is the first one to reach the finish.

Start

1 2 3 4 5 6 7 8 9 10 11 12 13 14 15

Play the game again. This time, start at the end and work backwards along the track.

Try this

Choose a book and look at the page numbers. Copy the numbers onto some paper. Can you read and write all the numbers up to 40?

16 17 18 19 20 21 22 23 24 25 26 27 28 29 30

Finish

Place value

Throw a coin onto the spinner. Take that number of counters and put them on the Ones planet. When you have 10 counters on the Ones planet, take these away and put one counter on the Tens planet. Say each time how many tens and how many ones you have, then say the whole number. Keep going until you have 2 counters on the Tens planet.

Tens

Do this again. This time go to 3 Tens.

spinner

1	2
4	3

Challenge

You will need some playing cards.
Take out all the picture cards.
Shuffle the rest of the cards.
Say any number between 10 and 40.
Now use the cards to
make the number.

36

Ones

Counting patterns

Start at 0. Count along the track in twos.
Which numbers do you say?

Start
0
1
2
3
4
5
6
7
8

What if you counted in 5s? And 10s? And 3s?
Write a list of the numbers that you say.

Find out

What if you counted in 2s starting on 14 and ending on 26? What numbers would you say? Now count back in 2s from 28 to 18. What numbers would you say? Now try counting on in 5s from 10. How far can you count?

14, 16, 18, 20...

9 10 11 12 13 14 15 16 17 18 19 20 Finish

13

Odds and evens

The gardener planted some flower bulbs in even numbers. The rabbits ate some of the bulbs. Which rows have an even numbers of flowers?

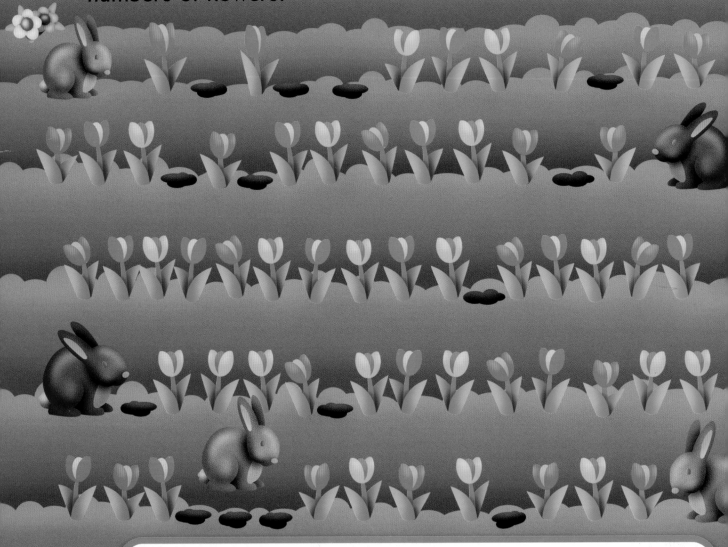

Add 1 to the number of flowers in each row.
Now which rows have even numbers of flowers?

15

Making comparisons

Decide which home has more in each pair of sets below.
Say how many more there are.

Count each set of animals below:

Say the number that is 1 more.

Say the number that is 1 less.

Say the number that is 10 more.

Say the number that is 10 less.

Now try this

Choose a page in this book between 11 and 24. Say its page number. Now say these numbers: 1 more, 1 less, 10 more and 10 less. Try this again for another page. You could write your numbers down.

15
16, 14
25, 5

Ordering numbers to 20

Look at the lines of numbers. The numbers are in order, but the bears have dropped paint onto some of the numbers. Which numbers have paint on them?

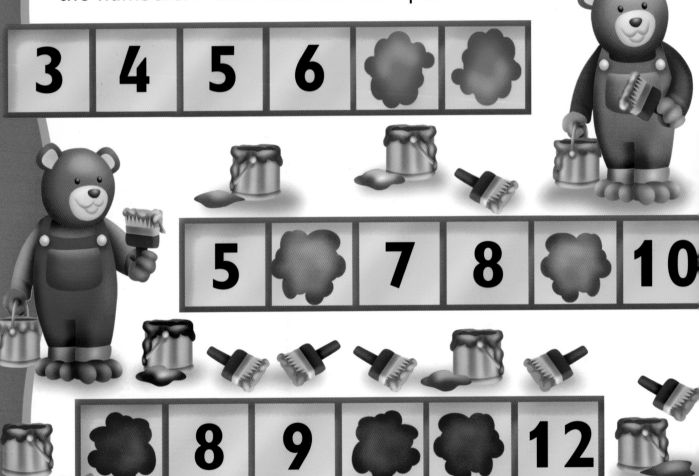

2 of the number grids on these pages could be placed together to make a longer line of numbers in order. Which grids are those? Write the numbers down in order.

Challenge

You will need some playing cards. Take out all the picture cards. Choose 2 cards. Put them in number order. Now say a number which would fit between your numbers.

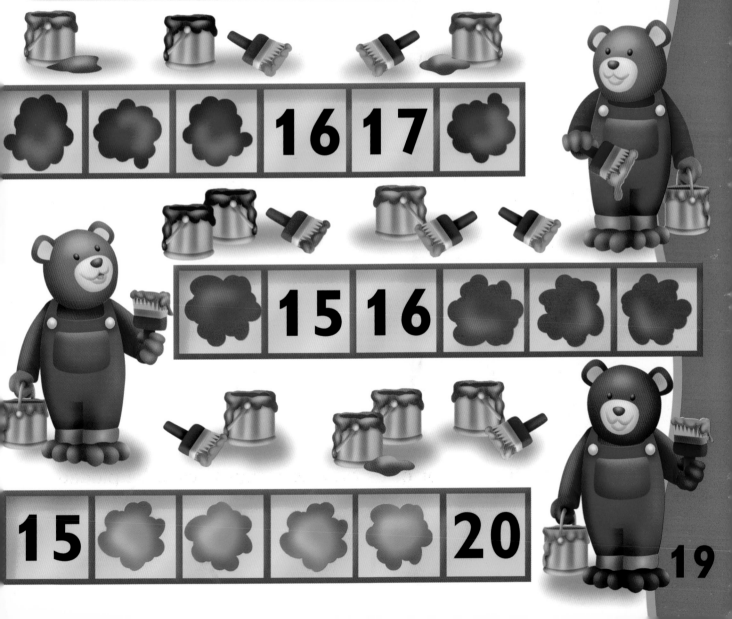

16 17

15 16

15 20

19

Number problems

You will need some counters in two different colours. Jump your finger along the track in 2s. Put a counter on each number that you touch. Do this again for jumps of 3s. Write a list of the numbers that have 2 counters on them. What is special about these numbers?

Start

1
2
3
4
5
6
7
8
9
10
11
12
13

Now try this

Jump along the track in 5s.
Put a counter on each number that
you touch. Now think about jumping
along the track in 2s. Can you
guess which numbers would be
touched by jumps of both 2 and 5?

5, 10, 15…

2, 4, 6, 8, 10…

Finish

16 17 18 19 20 21 22 23 24 25 26 27 28 29 30

14 15

21

Supporting notes

Counting to 20 – pages 4–5

Count with real objects at first, then move to counting pictures.
Extend this to counting sets to 30, then beyond. Try to use lots of different contexts.

Estimating – pages 6–7

Use different objects for estimating and counting, e.g. coins, cubes,
counters etc, so that the children experience estimating items of various sizes.
Try putting small things, such as marbles and buttons, into a transparent container, and
ask the children to estimate these. Use pictures in books. Give the children a few seconds
to look, then close the book and ask, 'How many… do you think there were?'

Numbers to 30 – pages 8–9

Provide opportunities for reading and writing numbers up to at least 30,
such as finding page numbers in books; reading numbers on packaging;
prices etc. Encourage the children to write the numbers in the air with
their arms, so that they 'feel' the shape that the numbers make.

Place value – pages 10–11

Exchange games can be played with coins, e.g. 1s and 10s coins.
Ask the child to take a handful of 1 coins and to count these out.
Then exchange 10 one coins for a 10 coin. Then ask, 'How much money
do you have?' Children can use playing cards to make TU (tens and units) numbers.
They read the number and say how many tens and how many units.

Counting patterns – pages 12–13

Practise saying the patterns for counting in 2s from 0 to 20 and back again.
Do this for 5s, 10s and 3s up to about 30. When children are confident
with this, they can say the patterns backwards, starting with 20, then 30.
Children may like to sing the counting patterns to music.

Odds and evens – pages 14–15

Where children are counting objects, they can pair these to see if
they are even (pairs with no odd ones) or odd (always 1 left over).
Encourage children to recognize that even numbers always have 0, 2, 4, 6 or 8
in their unit number, and that odd numbers always have 1, 3, 5, 7 or 9.

Making comparisons – pages 16–17

Children can compare numbers that they find around them,
such as numbers in books, on toys etc. They can say, of two numbers,
which is more/less, and what number(s) could fit between them.
Encourage them to say numbers that are 1 more/less than any number up
to 30, and for numbers between 10 and 20, numbers that are 10 more/less.

Ordering numbers to 20 – pages 18–19

Ask questions about number order such as, 'Which numbers could fit
between… and…?' If children are unsure, use some number cards so
that they can find the numbers they need and place these in order.

Number problems – 20–21

This number investigation encourages children to think about how some
numbers come in both the counts of 2 and of 3. This is the basis of the
6 times table, of course. If children find the jumping along the track difficult,
suggest that they use their fingers to keep track of each jump of 2 or 3.

Using this book

The illustrations in this book are bright, cheerful and colourful, and are designed to capture children's interest. Sit somewhere comfortable together as you look at the book. Children of this age will usually need to have the instructional words on the pages read to them. Please read these to them, then encourage them to take part in the activity.

In this book, children are encouraged to work both practically, by counting and using counters/tokens, and by working mentally, such as counting 'in their heads'. They are introduced to numbers to 30 and are expected to be able to read and write these numbers by the end of the book. You may want to extend this to numbers to 40, 50... if the children are confident with reading and writing numbers to about 30. As well as counting forwards, count back from larger numbers: 20, 19, 18... and 30, 29, 28... This will help the children to recognize where any of these numbers come within a counting sequence.

There are opportunities for counting in 2s, 3s, 5s and 10s. With practise at counting, children will begin to spot the patterns, so give plenty of opportunities for this. When counting in 2s, start on both 0 and 1, so that children can say the counting pattern of even numbers: 0, 2, 4, 6... and odd numbers: 1, 3, 5...

Children are introduced to the concept of place value. It is really important for children to understand that a digit's position in a number determines its worth. For example, 52 is not the same number as 25 or 520. Take opportunities to read two-digit numbers, such as 24, 13... and ask questions such as, 'What number is this? How many tens are there? How many units?' Ask the children to write the number down, then to write it down again, reversing the digits, such as 23 and 32 and ask, 'Are these the same number? Why not? How can you tell?'

Remember, learning about mathematics should always be a positive experience. So, enjoy together the mathematical games, activities and challenges in this book!